TALES OF THE CARIBBEAN

A MEMOIR

BOOK 1
OUR COMMUNITY

THE BEAUTIFUL
ISLAND OF BARBADOS

AUTHOR AND ILLUSTRATOR
ISABELLA CLARKE

To order additional copies of this book, contact:
Xlibris
1-888-795-4274
www.Xlibris.com
Orders@Xlibris.com

ISBN: Softcover 978-1-4797-8218-5
EBook 978-1-4797-8219-2

Print information available on the last page

Rev. date: 06/09/2020

DEDICATION

This book is dedicated to my loving children, Lucille, Walter, and Laurianne.

To Lucille, who went to City College, got the college application, and filled it out for me. She made sure that I returned it to the college in order to be accepted to start classes. She was determined that I get a college education because she saw me struggling. She knew that with a college education, I could get a better job and my life would be less stressful. She departed this life on March 15, 2009.

To my son, Walter, because he monitored and critiqued everything I said and did from his childhood. In his adult life, he often told me how much he admired my determination in pursuing and accomplishing my goals in life. I never knew that he was paying attention to how many times I took the State Board Teachers' Exam and failed it. He said to me, "But, Mommy, you never gave up." I told him, "We Pollards never give up." I told him that when I was a child, I was taught by my father and often saw my older brother, while doing his homework, standing in front of the mirror and reciting this poem: "Try, try, try, try again. If at first you don't succeed, try, try, try, try again." It encouraged him to pursue and accomplish his own educational goals, even when things got rough for him.

To Laurianne, who encouraged me to write. She said that because of my experience in working with children and teaching them, I need to write children's books. Both she and Walter said that I have a world of information in my head and a history of my upbringing in Barbados, West Indies, so I need to "write, write, write." Laurianne often said to me, "Mommy, don't think about the spelling or punctuation, just write whatever comes to you and the correct spelling and punctuation will be done when the story is being edited."

I also dedicate this book to the memory of my late husband, Elder Clyde E. Clarke, who departed this life on March 20, 2008. He has been a mentor and an inspiration in my life. His teaching and the example he set for me in the life that he lived helped me to be the person I am today. Whatever I told him I wanted to do in life, he encouraged me to follow my dreams. I really miss him.

Who is Isabella L-Clarke? She is the third living child of Mr. and Mrs. Walter and Rosalie Pollard. She was born in the island of Barbados, West Indies, in the 1940s. She lived in the village of Sea View in the parish of Christ Church with her parents and nine other siblings. Isabella was considered to be a very intelligent, curious, and adventurous child by her neighbors. She attended the St. Bartholomew's Anglican Church for her spiritual upbringing and the St. Bartholomew's Girls' School for her early childhood and elementary education. She started school at the age of three. She had to accompany and protect her oldest sister Albertina, who was born with infantile paralysis. Bertha, who was the oldest girl in the community, took the responsibility of overseeing and protecting all the children in the community on their way to and from school.

Isabella immigrated to New York City in June 1961. She worked in Head Start Early Childhood and day care programs while obtaining her formal education. After receiving her bachelor of science degree from the City College of New York, she worked as a paraprofessional in the New York City Department of Education public schools' system. She worked as a permanent teacher after receiving her master of science degree, her New York State Certification, and her New York City Certification in special education. She taught children with special needs for twenty-two years.

Isabella L-Clarke is a seamstress, a mother of three children, a grandmother of five, a great-grandmother of eight, and a great-great-grandmother of one. She is also an International Evangelist, an Elder in the church where she worships, and has been a retired teacher since July, 2007.

CONTENTS

INTRODUCTION 8

MY COMMUNITY: THE PEOPLE WHO LIVED THERE 10

HENRIETTA GOES FOR A WALK 17

DAILY LIVING IN THE COMMUNITY 19

OUR JOURNEY TO SCHOOL 19

OUR DAILY SCHOOL ROUTINE 24

OUR JOURNEY HOME FROM SCHOOL 27

THE FOODS WE ATE 32

FARM ANIMALS IN THE COMMUNITY 35

SEAFOOD HUNTING 42

THE GAMES WE PLAYED 44

MY FIRST VACATION TO AMERICA AND MY RETURN HOME . . . 46

ABOUT THE AUTHOR AND ILLUSTRATOR 47

ACKNOWLEDGEMENTS

For many years, I wanted to write. When I started working in day care, I wrote one page, which I called the beginning of my autobiography. Many times I read and reread it, not understanding how to write it.

When I started college at the Borough of Manhattan Community College in 1979, I was in a remedial reading class, which was being taught by a female professor. She said that she was originally from Guyana. I do not remember her name. I do remember her telling me that she does not see me sitting behind a computer all day working. She said that I was a person who would do better writing children's books. I was also taking a course in data processing at that time. My response to her was, "You don't know me, so how could you say that?" She said to me, "That is what you think." She went on to say that she is in front of the class teaching us every day and that she knows something about each one of her students. For many years, I have been jotting down different thoughts that came to me and different titles for stories. Many years later, I heard my children telling me, "Mommy, you need to write." Now, in the year 2012, after being retired for almost five years, I am getting ready to publish my first book.

At this time, I want also to acknowledge two of my professors: Dr. Johnson and Dr. Jiggets from the City College of New York. To Dr. Johnson because she took so much time and patience with me, teaching me how to do a research paper. She told us in the class that when she gets through with us, we will be able to write books and edit them ourselves. Recently I saw her and told her that I was writing a book. She told me that if I needed her help, I can always call on her and she will be happy to assist me.

To Dr. Jiggets, who encouraged me to write a comparison research paper on "the need for special education between Barbados and New York City." After reading many of my papers, he suggested that I should get them published because I wrote them very well.

INTRODUCTION

Hello, my name is Rosalie Isabella. I was named Rosalie after my mother and Isabella after my grandmother. In my family and in my community, they call me Isabella or Isa for short. Traditionally, this is how you carry on your family's names.

I was born and raised on the island of Barbados, West Indies, in a small village called Sea View, in the parish of Christ Church. I am the third living child of my parents, whose names were Walter and Rosalie. My brother Evan is the oldest child. My sister Albertina is the second child but the oldest girl. There is a total of ten children. Eurica is the fourth child, and Lavenia is the fifth. Walter is the second boy and the sixth child. His first name is Walter, after our father's first name, and his second name is after our grandfather's first name. After him are Loretta, Naomi, Elvira, and Elizabeth.

When I think back on my childhood years, I can only say that God has been so good to me. I was once a little girl, about eighteen months old it seems, as I visualized walking in the yard below our house. I was living there with my family. I remember hearing airplanes flying over my head. When I looked up, I saw groups of dark green airplanes flying toward the ocean. The first group was a group of three, [image] the second group of three, [image] with a total of about nine airplanes [image]. Three flew ahead of the others, each one making a dive, turning over, and then returning to position. The other airplanes did the same rotation over the ocean, and then they turned in a circular direction over the ocean and disappeared. People in the neighborhood said that the airplanes were warplanes.

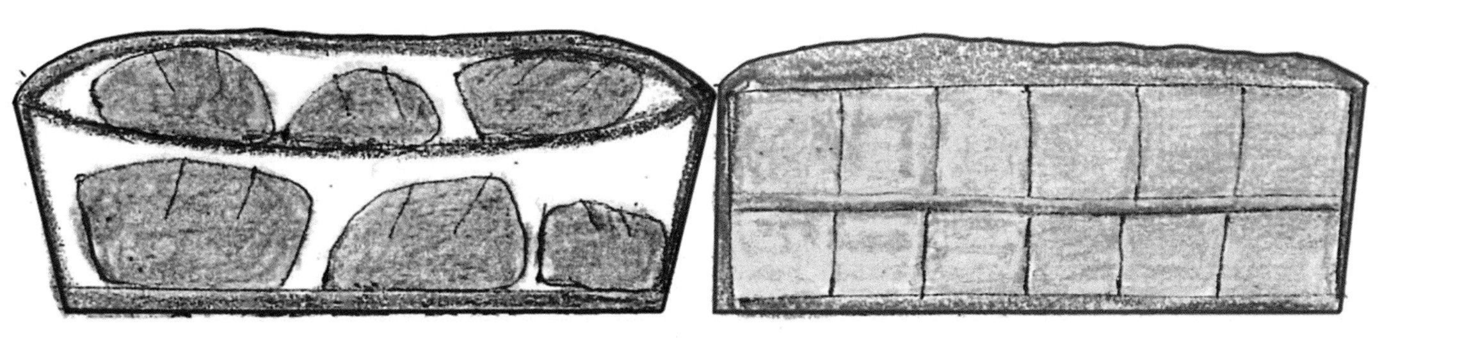

MY COMMUNITY: THE PEOPLE WHO LIVED THERE

In the village of Sea View, there were sixteen houses. In the first house across the lawn from our house was the home of Mr. & Mrs. Roberts. They had five children: Eurine—whom I believe was the oldest—Carla, Wilfred, Glenda, and Inez. Inez died at around twelve years of age. It was said by the older people that if a person in the community died and they were very close to the children, you should lift the children over the coffin back and forth so that the person does not return and take the children. I remember two adults standing, one on each side of the coffin, lifting my oldest sister Albertina and me over Inez's coffin three times during the funeral service. It was said that Eurine, at a later date, went to America. We did not see her anymore.

Across from Mr. & Mrs. Roberts house was the house of their son, William and his wife Marcia. West of their house lived Glenda, her husband, and their two children. Behind her house were Carla and her husband's house. Carla baked sweet bread [] and pone [], which she sold to the people in the neighborhood and to people who worked on the plantation.

North of Carla's house were Mr. & Mrs. Lewis. She made muffins [] and salt fish cakes [], to sell. Mr. Lewis kept a cow so they could get milk. North of Mrs. Lewis were Mr. John and his son. Mr. John bought and sold salt bread, [], and biscuits []. In front of their house was a dirt road leading up a hill. We called it the Long Hill. It led up to the district of Fairy Valley tenantry. East of Mrs. Lewis, and to the right of the walkway were Mr. & Mrs. Matthews. They kept a mule, which they used for transportation. Sometimes they bought and sold potatoes, yams, or eddoes from the plantation. Sometimes, when the factories were grinding sugarcane, the pressure of water in the community was very low. Sometimes the standpipe gave no water at all. Mr. Matthews took his mule with the cart to another neighborhood with a giant-sized can to fetch water. When he returned, he allowed his neighbors in the community of Sea View to get a bucket or two of water each.

To the left there was an old lady whose name was Ms Violet. She died when we were still quite young. During that time, when a person died, they were buried the next day. If you died early in the morning and your family could get the gravedigger to dig the grave before 4:00 PM, they would bury you on the same evening. There were no funeral parlors then that I knew of. The nurse came to the house and prepared the body for burial. The body was then placed in a box that someone built to bury you in. They called it a coffin. People in the neighborhood came and viewed the body. Sometimes the coffin would be placed on a mule cart to take the body to the church. Sometimes, if a person had a hearse and the family could afford to pay for it, they hired it to take the body to the church. The people in the community formed a procession and followed the hearse to the church. People from other communities met the procession along the way. Others met at the church for the service and burial. It was a long walk to the church. As the procession drew near to the church, the sextant would toll the church bell. As it got closer, the sextant would ring the bell without stopping until the whole procession entered into the church yard. The priest then came out to meet the body, leading it into the church as he read certain prayers. The body was carried by the pallbearers. Family members usually got flowers together and made wreaths. One they hung outside over the front door where the person lived, and one they placed on the coffin.

On the east of Ms Violet's house, near the gully that goes from north to south, was an old wall house. There, Mr. and Mrs. Bynoe and their two children lived. Coming back west in the district from Mr. John and traveling south, there was a narrow road going east in front of Carla's house leading behind another section of the gully that separated Mr. & Mrs. Roberts from Mr. & Mrs. Matthews. This section of the gully, East of Mr. & Mrs. Roberts house, connected to the gully running north and south, which ended on the bay of the ocean. This was down the hill from our house. The ocean also circled around, bordering where the schoolmistress lived.

On the west side of Glenda's house was a standpipe, with a road leading east and back In front of Mr. & Mrs. Robert's house and down the hill to the beach. Next to the standpipe was an old lady named Mrs. Barns. After her husband died, she had an adopted daughter and her five children living there with her. There were three boys and two girls. We all played games in the community together in the evenings when all our work was done. When the oldest child, a girl named Willma, left and went to England, their mother and the other children moved to another location. Mrs. Barns was left alone. She asked my parents if I could spend the nights with her. My parents agreed, and so I was able to spend the nights with her. She always left tea and biscuits for me at nights, but she wanted me to come early so that I could keep her company before we went to bed. Early the next morning, I would come home, have breakfast with my family, do my chores, and get ready for school.

On the east side of Mrs. Barns' house was the family of Mr, & Mrs. Bennett and son, Thomas. It is said that Mr. Bennett went to America. When he returned, he brought back a gramophone. That was a kind of record player. He also had large records. He was the only one in the community to play that kind of music. Some years later, most people in the community were able to acquire a radio called the Radio Fusion. That was a radio with only one station. It was connected by some kind of a wire in a high corner of the front house. It came on automatically every morning at 6:00 AM and signed off at 11:00 PM every night.

To the south of the road, there lived two sisters whose names were Ms Julie and Ms Mary. At the end of the road was a big wall house. That is where the headmistress of the St. Bartholomew's Girls' School, Ms Haynes and her sisters Ms Grace and Ms Minerva, lived. Ms Grace was a second grade teacher at the same school. Ms Minerva was a Sunday School teacher at the St. Bartholomew's Anglican Church. Most of the people in our community attended St. Bartholomew's Church, and the children attended 9:00 AM service and Sunday school at 3:00 PM. The other children attended the Pilgrim Holiness Church in the district of Fairy Valley, which was up the hill from Sea View.

MR. & MRS. MURRAY
MS HAYNES
BUSH AND TREES
SHEEP & PIGS' PEN
GOAT
COWS' PEN
THE POLLARD'S FAMILY HOUSE
FRONT LAWN
MS MARLENE
WORKING LAND
MR. JOHNSON
WORKING LAND
MRS. BENNET
ROAD
MS JULIE
MS MARY
MRS. BARNS
BEACH
GULLEY
MR. & MRS. BYNOE
MR. & MRS. MATTHEWS
MS. VIOLET
GULLEY
ROAD TO THE BEACH
ROAD
STAN
PIPE
GLENDA
CARLA
MR. & MRS. ROBERTS
WILLIAM &
MARCIA
MR &
MRS LEWIS
MR. JOHN
MAP OF SEAVIEW

TALES OF THE CARIBBEAN

Coming back into the district on the right-hand side, east of the road across from Ms Julie and Ms Mary, there were three other houses. Mr. & Mrs. Johnson lived in the nearest one. He was a fisherman with his own boat []. He caught different kinds of fish. Some they called pot fish. They were placed on strings in groups of six or more of different kinds and different sizes. The cost of the fish depended on the quantity of fish on the string []. Some he sold to the people in the neighborhood while others he sold to people in distant neighborhoods.

East of them were Ms Marlene, her husband and their five children. East of them, in the last house, were her parents. We, as children, were taught to call all female adults Miss or Missus. and male adults Mister, even if they were not married. We called them Mr. & Mrs. Murray. Mrs. Murray was a housewife, but during the Sea Eggs season, she would buy sea eggs from the fishermen. She seasoned and steamed them and took them to town and sold them. Mr. Murray was a fisherman. He mostly watched the beach on nights when the moonlight was shining bright to see when the turtles came to shore to lay their eggs []. He would get his sons to help him turn the turtles on their backs []. Since the turtles were so large, he would return early the next morning with other men from the neighborhood to help him. They then put the turtle into a bag each time he caught them. They would tie the bag to two poles, place the poles on their shoulders, and lift the turtles up the sea rocks, on the hill, to his home. He also brought up the turtles' eggs to share with the neighbors in the community. Mr. Murray would somehow be able to reach buyers to sell the turtles to. It was my understanding that sometimes the buyers bought the whole turtle. Sometimes they cut it up, took what they wanted, and left the rest. Mr. Murray would then sell what was left by the pound to the neighbors in the community. If any was left, people from the next district, Fairy Valley, would come and buy turtle meat when they heard. I don't remember ever eating turtle meat, but I remember eating turtle eggs. No matter how long you cooked them, they were still soft.

Mr. and Mrs. Murray had two sons: Randy and Glenroy. They also had five daughters: Ms Marlene, Bertha, Dorie, Darlene, and Eva. They had sheep, goats, pigs, turkeys, chickens, and rabbits. The sheep and goats were kept at nights in pens. During the daytime, they were taken out on pastures to graze on the green grass. The pigs were kept in their own pens. In order for them to get exercise, one end of a long rope was tied around their necks as they were let out of their pens. The other end was tied to an iron stake that was hammered into the ground. The rabbits, chickens, and turkeys were kept in their separate coops in the backyard. The rabbits were fed with the green slip or the vine from the sweet potato plants. The chickens and turkeys were let out of their coops every morning and fed with scratch grain and coarsely ground corn or rice. In the evening, they were gathered together, fed, and led back into their coops. This was the procedure done in each home by all who had domestic animals.

HENRIETTA GOES FOR A WALK

Henrietta was the name given to one of the turkeys. She loved to disappear from the group and walk across the ground to Mrs. Roberts' yard to visit her turkeys. Mrs. Roberts would fuss and fret. She felt that the neighbor's turkey came to eat what she was feeding her turkeys. One morning, Dorie and Eva noticed Henrietta leaving the group. They watched her and tried to get ahead of her. As they walked on each side of her, Henrietta ran fast right into Mrs. Roberts' yard. They were both afraid to go into Mrs. Roberts' yard to get Henrietta. Dorie, being the older of the two sisters, said to Eva, "Eva, go for Aunt's turkey." Eva just stood there. Dorie repeated her instructions. Eva just stood there watching Henrietta. Dorie said the third time, "Eva, why you don't go for Aunt's turkey?" Finally, Eva responded by saying, "And if we and them don't agree?" Mrs. Roberts was angry. She came out of her house and chased Henrietta out of her yard and back to Dorie and Eva. They both chased Henrietta back to their home.

DAILY LIVING IN THE COMMUNITY

In the community of Sea View, the mornings began, in most cases, with the parent waking up the children to do some chores before they went to school. Those consisted of some of the children going up the hill to the district of Fairy Valley to fetch water from the standpipe. This water was distributed for different purposes—the children each took their bath while the mother washed the clothes and cooked the food during the day. The other children had to take the animals out on the pasture and stake them out to graze. After that, they got dressed for school. Sometimes a child may have to gather firewood and assist the mother in making breakfast and lunch before going to school. Breakfast may consist of bakes and fish cakes or toasted biscuits and fish cakes, or salt bread with butter. For drink, you may have lemonade or mauby. After getting to school late sometimes, you got a beating from the schoolmistress or from the schoolmaster. Times were very rough for us then. If the mother was sick, or had a newborn baby, the oldest girl, or the one who could better help, had to stay at home from school to assist the mother.

OUR JOURNEY TO SCHOOL

We started on our journey to school every week, Mondays to Fridays, except on holidays. All the children in our community in Sea View left home around 8:00 AM in order to get to school in time. Children who had greater responsibilities which they did not complete in time left home a bit later. If the parent sent a note to the schoolmaster or schoolmistress explaining why you were late, you may be excused from getting a beating. Instead of walking to school in a relaxed mood with your friends, you had to run most of the way. There were no busses, no taxis, and no trains to take us to school. If you were fortunate enough to have a bicycle, you could not even ride it to school. You just had to walk. The bicycle would be used to go to lessons during the weekends or to run errands.

On our way from Sea View to school, we had to climb a long hill to the district of Fairy Valley in order to go to school. Sometimes we met up with other children who were also going to the same school. It was a long walk to school. The roads were between different fields of the plantation. Some were cornfields, eddoe fields, cassava fields, potato fields, and of course, sugarcane fields. There were plenty of worms crossing the roads from one field to another. When they finished eating the leaves off the different plants in one field, they crossed the road to another field. I was always scared of those creepy crawling worms, so I had to skip and jump over them to avoid crushing them. By the time I reached the main road to school, I was exhausted.

We walked by a pond on our way to and from school. After passing the pond, we arrived at Fairy Valley Yard. That was where the big plantation house was. We were not allowed to walk through the yard. We had to walk below the yard, where it was wet and muddy when it rained. It also gave a terrible odor because the horses were kept in the yard. As we stepped onto the main road, there was a large tamarind tree on the right-hand side of the road that hung over the road. Farther down the road on the same side lived an old lady named Ms Paul. She had a large plum tree below her house. About twelve feet below her house was a blacksmith's shop. We often watched the blacksmith as he heated an iron and shod the iron shoe on the horses' hoofs. On the opposite side of the street, there was a shop. Sometimes, if any of the children had money, we would stop at the shop to buy candy or bread. Below the shop was a house owned by Ms Drake. She had a large achee tree—that is a fruit tree. Sometimes we picked achees from her tree and sometimes she gave them to us. Below her was the St. Bartholomew's Boys' School. Back on the right-hand side of the road, there was a standpipe. If our feet were muddy, we would stop at the pipe and wash our feet before going on to school, or if we wanted water to drink, we would drink water.

Ms Haynes, our schoolmistress, would stand upstairs of the school, on the platform by her desk, and look through the window. She watched to see who stopped at the shop or the standpipe. She stood there until we got in the gap of the school. If we were late, she would call from the window, telling us to come upstairs so she could beat us for stopping at the shop or at the pipe. If we were not late, we would line up on the lawn with our class when the school bell rang. The teachers would lead their classes by grade into the school building on the lower level. There, all the classes met for morning prayers and devotion. We also sang a hymn and recited a scripture. Sometimes we were given a new hymn or scripture to learn at home. Infants A and B, classes 1, 2, and 3 stayed downstairs. Classes 4, 5, 6, and 7 went upstairs.

OUR DAILY SCHOOL ROUTINE

During our daily routine at school, we were taught reading, writing, arithmetic, dictation, music, composition, history, geography, social studies, and home economics. In home economics, we learned cooking, how to fold table napkins, and how to set the table for breakfast, lunch, and dinner. We were taught good table manners. The teacher's motto was "Clean as you go." That meant, as soon as you finish using a dish, clean it and put it away. She said that it prevented you from having a sink full of dirty dishes and other utensils to wash when you finished cooking and eating. Each student had to wear an apron during cooking class. When the lesson was over, some students were assigned to wash the aprons; some were assigned to wash the towels. Some washed the dishes; some cleaned the kitchen, and some packed away the dishes and the utensils. Some days, when we did not cook, we were taught how to sew handkerchiefs, pillowcases, and aprons. We also learned how to do embroidery and make baskets and hats from the dried leaves of the wild cane lily plants. We call it wild cane. Sometimes we used part of a sack we called crocus bag to make mats. We used strips of different colorful fabrics. We each took a nail, placed the point in the center of the fabric, pushed it through from top to bottom for about half an inch, and pushed it back to the top. We then tied it in a knot. We repeated the same procedure until the class was over for that day. Each week, we continued the same procedure until the mat was finished. We were given the mats to take home for our parents. Mostly, our mothers would take the mat and place it at the front door inside of the house, especially at Christmastime. In later years, sometimes it may be an aunt who was caring for the child and had a car. She would take the mat and place it on her bathroom floor or use it to decorate the back window of her car.

When it came to music, certain children from the higher classes were selected to learn music. They were taken into a separate room with the music teacher who tested their voices. The teacher drew the music lines on the blackboard, drew the treble cleft, and then filled in the notes representing the scale. The children were then asked individually to identify the notes as the teacher pointed to them. The children sang the notes as a group and then individually. When the children learned the songs very well, some of these songs were selected and entered into competition with children from other schools. Whichever school won the competition went on to a higher competition with other children throughout the island of Barbados.

Sometimes there was an announcement made that the Queen of England, or some of the royal family, was coming to visit Barbados. Children from other schools were selected to sing in a choir at the Garrison Savannah to join in the celebration and, hopefully, to get a glimpse of the Queen or the royal family. There were so many adults who were larger than the children that the children could not see what was going on. On the day that the Queen was leaving Barbados to return to England, all the children had to wear their uniforms to school. Our uniform was a navy blue jumper with a white bodice, black shoes, white socks, and a red belt if you did not have a navy blue band around your waist. You also had to wear a red ribbon in your hair. Sometimes, children who never wore shoes, socks, or ribbons to school had to wear them that day. Children had to line up on the pasture above the school waving the Union Jack, which is the flag of Great Britain or England. As the Queen was driven by, we had to wave the flag and say, "All hail Royal Highness." At the boys' school, they had to wave white handkerchiefs as the motorcade passed by; it went so fast that we did not believe that the Queen even saw us. Prince Charles was about nine years old at that time.

When Princess Margaret visited Barbados, we had to learn and sing the song, "All hail Royal Highness, / How glad and proud are we, / of this, your visit, / to the aisle of the Caribbe. / We of Barbados, our loyal voices raise, / for us this always will remain, / a glorious day of days. / Our heartfelt prayer we offer, / that providence may bless, / your royal house, / your royal self, / with peace and happiness. / How great a privilege and honor it has been, / that we today should welcome, / the sister of our Queen."

During our history lessons, we learned about the discovery of the "Gunpowder Plot" in the United Kingdom. We were told that November 5 was known as Guy Fawkes Night, or Bonfire Night. We were taught that it represented the Gunpowder Plot of November 5, 1605, in which a number of Catholic conspirators, including Guy Fawkes, allegedly attempted to blow up the Houses of Parliament in London, England. Since the Gunpowder Plot failed, November 5 was celebrated each year as the anniversary with fireworks. Since Barbados, at that time, was still under the rule of Great Britain, we also celebrated Guy Fawkes Night. We also had a smaller celebration on November 25. As we lit the star lights and threw them into the air, we yelled, "The fifth of November, Guy Fawkes Night!" On the twenty-fifth, as we lit and threw the star lights in the air, we yelled, "The twenty-fifth of November!"

One year, on the night of November 5, the older children in our community were allowed to participate in the fireworks celebration with adult supervision. Mom gave each child at least two star lights, a rocket, and a bomb. The star lights were made of wire about nine inches long with gray sulfur on two-thirds of it on one end. The other end was left blank so you could hold it and throw it up in the air after lighting it. When it fell to the ground, you would then pick it up and throw it up again until it stopped sparkling and the light went out. She held the youngest child in her hand as she lit the star light. She then placed it in the youngest child's hand. She placed her hand over the child's hand for safety. As the starlight burned, it gave off sparkles like stars. Then she made circles in the air as she talked with the child, explaining what it was. Sometimes the child was afraid, and Mom had to take the star light and throw it in the air herself or give it to another child.

The bomb was something like a sulfur ball wrapped in paper, like a lollipop without the stick. When you threw it on a solid rock, it exploded and sounded like a bomb. When you lit the rocket up and you placed it on the ground, it shot up in the air and gave off lights like rainbow colors. The older children went with the adults in an area over the sea rocks for the last part of the fireworks. That consisted of burning old car tires. The smoke was thick and black. Mrs. Murray had steamed her sea eggs that night on an outdoor fire. The soot from the black smoke caused her sea eggs to be black on the top, so she could not take them to town to sell them that night. Some people made conkies as part of the celebration. They also called them stewed dumplings. During the fireworks activity, we ate conkies.

Coming back to the school activities—at the end of the week, the higher grades had to take the desks out on the school yard, and scrub them. They were given soap, a scrub brush, and something called EC. This was like bleach, which was used to get the ink stains out of the desks. You had to fetch the water from the pipe in the school kitchen and take it out on the yard. After the desks were dried, you took them back into the school and placed them in their correct places. Sometimes children switched desks if they did not like the one they had. When you finished class 7, it was considered the end of your elementary education. The boys were sent by their parents to learn joiner trade with an adult in another neighborhood. They learned to make chairs and benches of different kinds. The girls were sent to learn sewing with an adult, if they were interested in sewing. They learned to make their own clothes. They made petticoats, panties, pajamas, and of course, their own dresses. They eventually used that skill to earn money by making clothes for other people in their own community. Some girls were sent to private lessons to learn shorthand and typing. They used that skill to obtain jobs, such as doing secretarial work. Other students, mostly girls, went for training at a nursing school or cooking school with the hope of gaining a certificate. This allowed them to apply to the government for jobs in England or Canada under government contracts. If they were successful, they were allowed to travel to England or Canada to acquire jobs. Once they acquired jobs, if the government paid their passage to Canada or England, they had to pay the government back.

If parents wanted their children to attend secondary schools, in those days, the schoolmistress or schoolmaster gave the students each a letter of recommendation to take the Common Entrance Exam. The students had to be at least nine years of age. During that time, parents had to pay tuition, except for the children who won a scholarship. Parents who had several children could not afford to send them to a secondary school. After completing elementary school at around fourteen or fifteen years of age, the oldest girl child usually stayed at home to assist the mother with household chores.

OUR JOURNEY HOME FROM SCHOOL

On our journey home from school, we often stopped by Ms Paul's house to get some plums from her plum tree. Ms Paul was very fretful. She would chase the children from under the plum tree, except if they were with her nieces. When we got farther up the road, those of us who could climb a tree would climb the tamarind tree as high as we could go. Each person would pick tamarinds and drop them down to their sisters or other relatives below. When we came down from the tree, we would share the tamarinds. Once again, we had to walk below Fairy Valley yard in order to get home from school. We sometimes climbed up on a wall, which measured about four feet tall at the beginning and about six feet high at the end. It was about twelve feet long and about twelve to eighteen inches wide. We walked on the top of it for about twelve feet and then jumped off. After that, we walked a little farther and arrived at the pond. We often watched the frogs and tadpoles as they swam in the water. Sometimes we threw little pebbles into the water to see who could make the largest circles.

After passing the pond, we came to the sugarcane fields. If the sugarcane was being harvested and our friends' parents were working in that field, they would save us pieces of sugarcane, or we would walk where the sugarcanes were already picked up and sent to the factory to find pieces of sugarcane for ourselves. We could only do that if the manager or the bookkeeper was not there. Sometimes we ate the sugarcane before we reached home, trying not to soil our clothes. If it was a potato patch where the potatoes were already reaped, we would search to see what we could find. Sometimes we found a sprout, and we dug it up, finding a large potato or several small ones. We took them home and roasted them in the fire as our mother cooked the food. Sometimes we got enough potatoes for our mom to cook a meal. If not everyone had their own, we shared.

After arriving home from school, we had more chores to do. After dinner, some of us had to walk up the hill to the district of Fairy Valley to fetch more water. We mostly went in a group with our neighbor's children. Sometimes we had to climb the hill four times in order to bring four buckets of water. Then we had to go up the pasture to bring home the animals. Sometimes it was raining, but we had to go through the rain. Sometimes it was stormy weather with high winds and hard rain. We still had to go through it to bring home the animals. If there was a flood, the rainwater came flooding through the gully, cutting a wide path through the sand on the beach and running into the ocean. If the sea was rough and the waves were breaking high, it would cut away the sand on the other side, making a drop of about six feet deep. The seawater would also run over the sand, meeting the floodwater coming from the gully.

One evening, I had to go down to the beach and walk on the strip of sand because the floodwater had risen. I could not cross on the short side to climb the hill to get my father's cows. I had to cross the sand through the ocean water and cross back through the water coming from the gully as it was gushing into the ocean in order to bring home my father's cows. After gathering the cows together from the pasture and arriving back on the beach, the water from the gully had risen even higher. It was about three feet high and about six feet wide. The cows did not want to cross. I was the only human being there, and I had to get home with the cows. First, I prayed and asked God to help me to cross safely. Then, I took the rope of the two cows, stepped into the water, and began to pull the cows. The water reached up to my waist as it gushed toward the ocean. I pulled and pulled the ropes until the cows got into the water. They began to walk until we all got out of the water and onto the sand. If I had fallen into the water, I would have been washed into the ocean by the floodwater. Now, we were all on the strip of sand between the high rushing waves and the high gushing waters from the gully. We still had to walk on the sand to the west side of the bay and then climb another hill to get to our house. Finally, we made it home. I then had to tie the cows in their pen and change my wet clothes. In a case like that, to prevent my getting sick, my mom rubbed me down with Limacol. Then she gave me some hot tea with a little rum or brandy in it to drink. I thanked God that he brought me home safely.

THE FOODS WE ATE

In most cases, we ate the vegetables and ground provisions that we grew in our own land. We cooked and ate potatoes, corn, pumpkins, yams, eddoes, cassava, green plantains and bananas, beets, carrots, string beans, and okras. Sometimes we ate the raw tomatoes, cucumbers, and even okras as we picked them fresh off the vine. We peeled and ate the sugarcane. Sometimes the plantation sold yams, cassava, potatoes, eddoes, or peas. Most of the people who worked there bought as much as they had money to buy before the plantation sold any to the outsiders. Sometimes, if you did not have any more of what you grew in your own land, you would buy from the plantation. People who worked at the sugarcane factory brought home syrup and hard lumps of sugar, which they did not want at the factory. They also were given crack liquor, which was the first stage of grinding the sugarcane. The second stage was sweet liquor; the third stage was syrup, which was made thicker than the first. The fourth stage was even much thicker and darker. They called it molasses. The fifth stage was sling. It was also thick but much lighter in color. The sixth stage was the dark brown sugar. After that, they began to refine the sugar and made it lighter.

Parents who had many children did not always have something to cook. They sent one or two of their children to another family member's house to ask for something to cook. That family member would send some of whatever they had bought from the plantation, along with any food that they had already cooked. Sometimes parents bought rice, a coconut, and some sugar from the store. They broke open and grated the coconut, boiled some of it into the pot of water with the rice, and added some cinnamon, nutmeg, clove, and bay leaves to flavor it. When the rice was cooked very tender, they added fresh milk or condensed milk and sugar, according to the sweetness that the parent wanted it to be. Then it was served as a hot cereal.

They called it rice tea. That was dinner for the evening. Sometimes they used cornmeal or oatmeal with the same recipe. The cornmeal cereal, they called pap. Sometimes they may have had dried cocoa or chocolate beans that someone gave them. They would get a medium-sized, smooth, round, or oval rock, clean it, and place the beans on the center of the flat rock. With the smaller rock, an adult gently crushed the beans small enough so it stood firm on the larger rock. Then they gently ground the beans into a fine powder. They sifted the powder and then rolled some into small balls. Some they rolled in a long shape like sticks and placed them to dry so they could last a long time. They ground the coarser powder and boiled it, making hot chocolate. Sometimes they mixed flour with sugar, spices, and water, and made dumplings without baking powder, which they cooked in the boiling chocolate. They called it "hot chocolate and flour drops." That was another evening meal. Sometimes the shopkeeper had leftover salt bread, which was a bit hard. He/she sold it at a reduced price. Sometimes he/she would give some to parents who had many children. The mother was thankful. She would take the bread, cut it in pieces, and dip some of it in hot chocolate, milk, or tea to soften it. They would have it for breakfast. Sometimes the mother used some of the same bread that is cut up to make bread pudding. She would place it in a clean, greased baking pan. Then she added some raisins, beaten eggs, milk or water, cinnamon, nutmeg, vanilla essence, and a sprinkle of sugar. She placed it in the oven to bake for about half an hour or until golden brown. This bread pudding was served as dessert or served during the day as a snack. Neighbors helped each other in every way. They also attended to each other's children in the community.

FARM ANIMALS IN THE COMMUNITY

Each family in our community kept farm animals. Each child had a sheep or a goat, and some had chickens. The father may have had cows to give milk. When Christmas or Easter time came, an animal may be sold in order to buy clothes or special groceries for that occasion. The butcher buying the animal may kill it on the premises. After taking what he wanted, he sold some parts to the neighbors and to whom he bought the animal from. He may leave the belly and the head so the neighbors can clean it and divide it among themselves to cook. They used lime, salt, and vinegar to clean and purify it. They often made soup with it. They got together and cleaned the pig's belly. Then they divided it. Some made a stuffing of seasoned, grated sweet potatoes, colored with burnt sugar or blood from the pig. They called it black pudding. They thoroughly cleaned and cooked the pig's feet and ears. Then they added seasoning, which we now call scallion, thyme, chopped onions, salt, and chopped red hot pepper. Then they let it stay in a dish to marinate with vinegar. After that, they served it with bread or other ground provisions. For most people in Barbados, that was their Saturday afternoon's meal. They called it black pudding and souse.

Some people choose special parts of the animal, depending on what money they had. A person may ask for a leg of lamb or a shoulder. Some wanted the ribs, the breast, or the loin. Some people took parts of the meat and ground it with an iron hand grinder. They called the meat minced meat. This minced meat was used to make minced meat pies or patties. The parts with the most meat were most expensive. After cleaning and seasoning it, they cooked it in an iron pot with a little oil until it was brown and tender. They called it potting the meat. This was also done with pork or beef.

Sometimes parents may kill a chicken, a duck, or a rabbit that they raised themselves. They purified it with lemon, salt, and vinegar. Then they would process the meat in the same manner. They may stuff the whole chicken or duck with seasoned bread crumbs or stale bread. Then they potted it, or they cut up the chicken in smaller pieces and fried it. When flying fish was in season and plentiful, each child may get one or two whole fried fish for himself. Sometimes the fish would be steamed. The older children helped the mother clean and bone the fish. As a reward, they got the fish rows and melts on the side to fry for themselves. Today they call it caviar and sell it at a high price.

Children at that time appreciated whatever was given to them. They were happy and contented. Sometimes you had to buy salted fish from the shop. You had to soak and then boil it in order to get most of the salt out of it. You then fried it with onions, tomatoes, and other seasonings, and made gravy with it. That was your meat with rice or cou-cou. Sometimes you cooked sweet potatoes, pumpkin, yams, and eddoes or cassava. The gravy was served over the ground provisions. They called it steamed food. Sometimes people cooked the salted fish with okras and other vegetables and called it callaloo. Everyone was happy they had something to eat.

People in those days did not have running water in their homes. They did not have electricity or refrigerators. In most cases, they cooked enough food each day for that day. If any dry foods such as rice, potatoes, or fried meats were left over, they were saved and heated for breakfast the next morning. Any soup or cereal would turn sour. In that case, it would be mixed with what they called feed and fed to the pigs. Everything you had was used for a purpose. Nothing was wasted.

For cooking utensils, most people used a three-legged iron pot. In this case, you used rocks on three sides of the pot, set about six or eight inches from the base. Wood was collected for the fire. The fire was lit under the pot of water to cook the food. Sometimes the mother mixed a pudding. I watched my mother as she mixed sugar and butter in a bowl with several spices. She added beaten eggs as she continued stirring it. She alternately added flour and milk or water. Sometimes, if she had raisins, she added some. When she got a smooth, moist consistency, she washed and greased a tall pan and put the mixture into the pan. She then placed the pan into the pot of boiling water, covered it, and let it cook for about half an hour or more, checking it at intervals until it was finished. People called it steam pudding. Sometimes a coal pot was used inside the house to cook the food if it was raining outside. Some people were fortunate and were able to buy a kerosene stove to cook on. They also bought an oven to sit on top of the stove burner when they wanted to bake. The outside kitchen may not have had a roof. They called it a fire hearth.

Children coming from school did not know whether or not there was food at home when they arrived. They often gathered fruits from many different fruit trees. They ate some on their way home from school and took some home to share with their family. Many of these fruit trees grew wild. Some grew around people's houses, mostly in their backyards. They were the sugar apple, the golden apple, soursop, guava, dunks, cherries, sea grapes, achees, turkey plum, fat pork, yellow plums, avocadoes, mangoes, oranges, gooseberries, wild cucumbers, and cashew. They even picked limes to make lemonade at home. One other thing we grew was sorrel. Sorrel grows as a red-stemmed plant with green and red leaves. It has thick red flowers that are hard and juicy with a round white pod in the middle of the flower. Inside of each pod are several seeds. At harvest time, which is mostly around Christmastime, the plants are cut down, the flowers are cut off, and the petals are cut from the pod and put to dry. The petals are then put in a container with hot or boiling water with cinnamon, nutmeg, and clove or other spices to steep. Some people keep it that way for about one week before straining the red liquid off. By that time, it has a beautiful aroma and the strength of the sorrel. It is then sweetened, mostly with brown sugar, and served as a Christmas drink. Some people just let it steep for a few hours, prepare it the same way, and serve it as hot or cold tea. It is red and looks like Kool-aid.

Sometimes family members or neighbors, having any of these fruits, gave them to the children to take home to their parents when they were ripe. Children, at an early age, learned how to be concerned about each other's needs and to share whatever they had with each other.

When gooseberries were plentiful, mothers worked together with their children to make gooseberry jam. They washed the gooseberries and placed them in a pot to boil with sugar and water. They added lemon or orange peel, cinnamon, nutmeg, and cloves for flavoring.

Sometimes they added ginger. They cooked it until it was thick and well done. Then it was put to cool. Most of the time, the seeds were removed. Everyone got a chance to taste it. The jam was placed in clean glass jars. The gooseberry jam was used on bread or crackers as a sandwich. The same recipe applied to cherries, guavas, and golden apples. The same procedure was used to make jelly with the same fruits, with the exception of the sugar being placed to boil and melt first until the sugar was very thick. Then the fruits and flavors were added while constantly stirring until the mixture was smooth. It was then strained to get the seeds out. When it was cooled, the mixture was then poured into jars and labeled. We called it homemade jelly or homemade jam. Sometimes they used the orange peel or grapefruit peel with the outer peel cut off. They sliced it and boiled it in the first water, which they threw off to prevent it from being too bitter. They added sugar and other spices to make preserve or marmalade. Sometimes people took sugar and coconut and boiled it with different spices and ginger until it was thick and sticky. Then they spoon-dropped the mixture and let it cool. They called it sugar cake or coconut candy. You see, we used many different fruits and vegetables to create many different foods. Children in their homes were taught these many skills.

SEAFOOD HUNTING

Seafood hunting was another skill. The older children from each household in the community assembled together on weekends, and sometimes during the summer vacation to search for seafood. They were accompanied by one or two adults from the community who supervised them. The assignment was to go to the beach when the seawater was low and receded. There, you walked on the sand and searched the rough rocks where the seawater waves normally beat. There, you found whelks and mussels stuck to the rocks. Sometimes you picked them off easily, and sometimes you had to use a rock with a sharp point to dig them off the rocks. After being there for about half an hour to one hour, whatever each person had, they took home to their parents. The mother would set a pot of water on the fire to boil. Then she would dump the whelks and mussels in the boiling water with salt to cook. After they were cooked and cooled off, the mother and the children worked together, cleaning them. They had to take the mussels and whelks out of their shells. The mother then chopped onions, thyme, and sometimes pepper and other seasonings, fried them together with a little flour, added some butter and water, and made gravy. This was distributed over whatever food she cooked. It was enough for everyone to receive a portion.

Some days during vacation time, the same group went to the beach. This time, they went into the area called the swamp. This is where the seawater came in when the sea was high and the water settled. Sometimes the rain fell and added more water. The area looked like a pond. Somehow, fish lived in it. We all walked quietly into the water and caught the fish with our bare hands. We placed them in sacks or pails, which we took to place the fish in. Whatever we caught, we took home. If a person did not catch any fish, the leader of the group would discuss with the group, and everyone shared.

The third thing we did was to hunt for land crabs—they came out when the moon shone brightly. The crabs were very large. They also lived in the swamp but on dry land. They dug very deep holes in the sand and lived there. In order to catch them, we took sacks and pails. We also took strong sticks with sharp points. The art of catching the crabs was, when you saw the crab and it was far away from its hole, you placed the pail over it. The adult then came with the opened sack, placed the mouth of the sack next to the pail, and lifted a part of the pail high enough for the crab to crawl out and into the sack. The adult then tied the mouth of the sack so that the crab could not escape. If the crab ran down into the hole before you caught it, you used the stick to push down farther back of the hole to stop the crab from going all the way. The crab would crawl back out of the hole. The adult then threw the sack over the crab and used the stick to push the crab into the sack. These were survival skills that we were taught in order to use resources from the land.

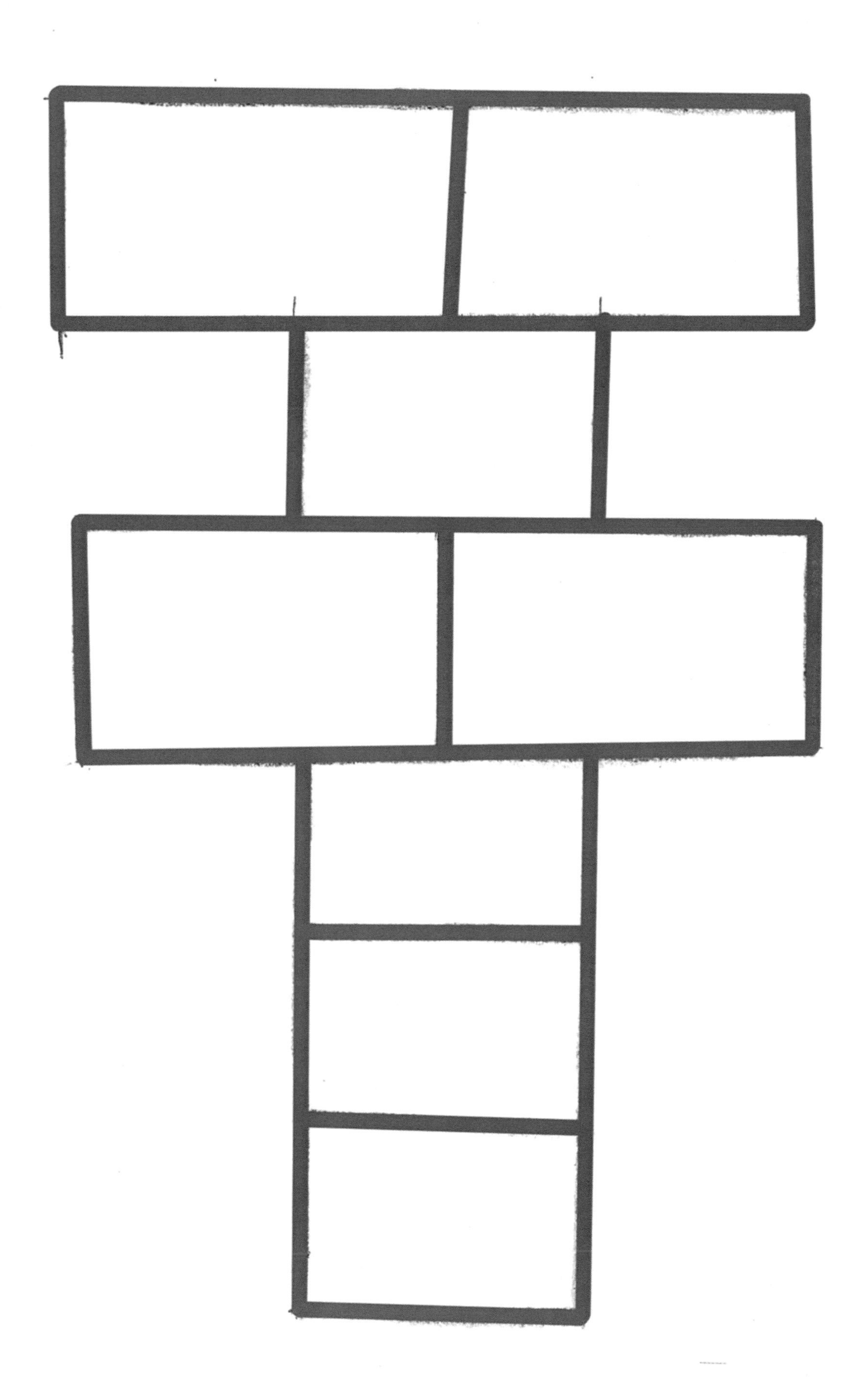

GAMES WE PLAYED

In our community, there were many games we played. After finishing our dinner and our chores, we were allowed to go outside to play. We had to play where our parents could see us.

One of the games we played was hopscotch. It was a diagram drawn on the ground. Three squares were connected together in one line, one on top of the other, followed by a wide rectangular shape. This rectangle was divided in half, being centered on top of the three single squares. One single square was drawn on top of the twin squares in the center, in line with the three individual squares at the bottom. Another rectangular shape was drawn and divided in half to match the twin squares below. Any number of players could play the game. Each person picked which number place he/she wanted to play. Each person then selected a piece of flat object to play the game with. In most cases, it was a smooth piece of broken glass of different colors or shapes, or even a bottle top. The first player began by throwing his/her object into the first square and jumping over it into the second square on one foot, without letting that foot touch any of the lines. He then jumped into the next square on one foot. To jump on the double squares, you used both feet, then one foot in the next single square, and both feet into the next double squares. You then turned around in the same double squares, facing the beginning of the diagram without your feet touching the lines. You reversed the jumping pattern until you reached the second square. You bend over, pick up your object, and jump out of the diagram.

In the second step, you throw the object into the second square; you jump into the first square, then jump over the second square, and follow the rest of the pattern. When you reach the double squares, you throw the object into one of the squares, follow the pattern of jumping, then you skip that square and keep on jumping until you reach the top. You turn around and continue jumping until you reach where your object is. You pick up your object and continue jumping until you reach the end. When you have completed all the squares without touching any of the lines, the game is over. If at any time you touch a line, you are out. If at any time your object rolls out of the diagram or if you threw in a square that you threw before, you are out. The second person gets a chance to play. When your turn comes again, you must start from where you stopped. The game goes on until everyone has had a chance to play. Then the game is over. If you only have two to four players, you have a better chance of playing the game of hopscotch more than once. I hope that by following these instructions, you will be able to play the game of hopscotch successfully if you never played it before.

Another game we played was hide-and-seek. If there are four players in the game, one player becomes the captain or the finder. The other players seek a place to hide as the finder covers his/her eyes with his/her hands. The finder counts loudly from one to three and say, "Ready or not, here I come." Since our community in Sea View was in the country, there were many trees or shrubs where we could hide. Our homes were also called chattel houses, which were built with an open cellar. The houses may have been built about three feet from the ground. At each corner of the house and in the middle were the strongest rocks for the solid foundation. Other solid rocks and the strongest soft stones were used to build around to fill in the foundation, leaving open spaces where you could crawl under the house. They called that the cellar. Under the cellar, you were allowed to play house. Certain areas were used to store firewood and other things. Under the cellar was also used as an outdoor place to hide without getting into trouble with your parents. If the player succeeded in finding all the players, that part of the game was over, and another person would be the finder. The game would continue until each person got a chance to be the finder. Then the game was over.

Another game we played was "Hilly Billy shut your lap tight, tight." This game began with all the players sitting in a circle on the ground with their legs crossed, in what we would call "Indian style", except the leader. The leader stood with an object in his/her hand, which he/she had to hide the object in one of the player's lap. The player whom he tapped the shoulder had to find the object in the lap where it was hidden. That was the end of the game. It may be a short stick, a small rock, or a bottle top. He/she bent over with the object in his hand, attempting to place it in the lap of one of the players. He/she went all around the circle, putting his/her hand in each person's lap, saying, "Hilly Billy Shut Your Lap Tight, Tight," until he/she got back where he/she started. At that time, he/she walked away and said, "My master, come and find the mistress's golden ring," or "My mistress, come and find my master's golden ring." He/she selected someone from the circle to search the lap of each one until the object was found, then the game was over. The person who found the object had to start the game all over or choose someone else to start the game. If they did not want to continue that game, they started a different game.

In playing the game of "London Bridge Is Falling Down," you could play with any number of children, both boys and girls. Any two children may volunteer or be chosen to be head of the game. The two formed an arch with their hands touching in the air in front of them. The other children line up one behind the other, singing the song, "London Bridge is falling down, falling down, falling down, / London Bridge is falling down, my fair lady." At that time, the two children lower their hands from forming the arch which represented London Bridge, and traps the person. Then they rock the person back and forth as they continued to sing, "Take the key and lock her up, lock her up, lock her up, / Take the key and lock her up, my fair lady." Then they released that person and started the song all over again until everyone had a chance.

Sometimes the boys played by themselves. They pitched marbles or used spinning tops, which they made themselves out of wood. They often found an old rim of a bicycle wheel. They took the middle with the spokes out, got a piece of wire, bent the wire at the end, and then started rolling the wheel forward. The art of that was to guide the wheel with the wire to see how far and how straight they could go before stopping. Sometimes they even ran instead of walking. We also took the center of the vine that grew on the beach or on trees, stripped off the leaves, and then we used it as jump rope. There were many other games that we played, which we created using our bodies or by finding resources in the community.

MY FIRST VACATION TO AMERICA AND MY RETURN HOME

I left Barbados in June 1961 for a vacation to visit with my aunt Albertina, who lived in America. While I was there, I attended a business school for about one year. After graduating, I got married. Soon after that, I returned to Barbados to visit my family and the people of the community of Sea View, Christ Church. When I arrived there, I discovered that most of the people had moved out of the area. Some had moved to the district of Chancery Lane, which was about a mile west of Sea View, some had moved to the district of Fairy Valley, which was up the hill from Sea View, and some of the younger people had migrated to Canada, England, or America. Some of the senior citizens had died. The only house remaining at that time was the old schoolmistress's. I visited her. I discovered that she was blind. The worker told her who I was and that I came to visit her. She welcomed me in. I began to talk with her and to tell her of some of my experiences in America. I reminded her of how she used to beat her students and how she beat me. Her reply to me was, "Didn't it make you learn better?" I told her, "No. It only made me nervous." I told her how I got stuck with the algebra because the American way of working out the problems was different from the way we did it in Barbados, which was the British method. Some of the spelling was also different because in America, we used the Webster's Dictionary and in Barbados at that time, we used the Collin's Dictionary.

I returned to America and lived there for many years. During that time, I raised my family, acquired a higher level of education, established a career, and worked there for many years until I retired.

THE END

ABOUT THE AUTHOR AND ILLUSTRATOR

As an author and illustrator of her first book, Isabella felt that it would take someone who was born and who lived in the village of Sea View, Christ Church, in the era that she lived there, to be able to write the story and draw the illustrations as it was then.

Upon speaking to one of her younger sisters, her sister told her that what she wanted to write and draw was all in her head and that she would be better able to be the author and illustrator of her own book. Isabella wanted every detail written and illustrated exactly as it happened.

As an illustrator, Isabella remembered the many classes and workshops that she attended during her years in college and her teaching career. She also remembered how she participated in the art classes when the art teacher came into the classroom to teach her students. Using these observations, Isabella decided to be the illustrator of her first book.

Copyedited by Pamela Estalilla
Reviewed by Ryan Cortes